In a snowy village nestled between mountains, everyone was preparing for the Christmas Eve celebration. This year, the princess wanted to make the holiday magical for everyone.

I Am Princess Kind
A Christmas Tale of Warmth and Giving

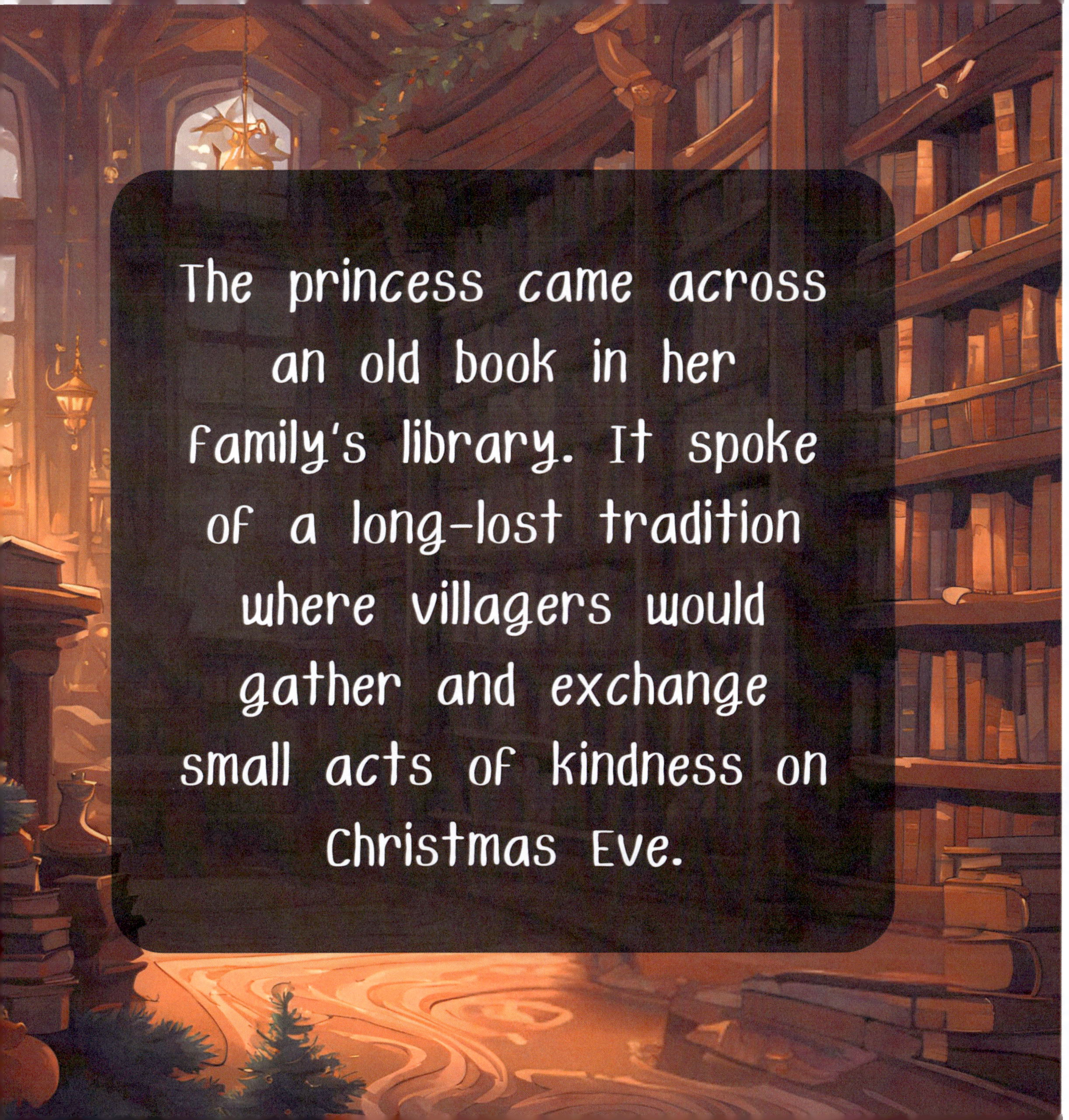

The princess came across an old book in her family's library. It spoke of a long-lost tradition where villagers would gather and exchange small acts of kindness on Christmas Eve.

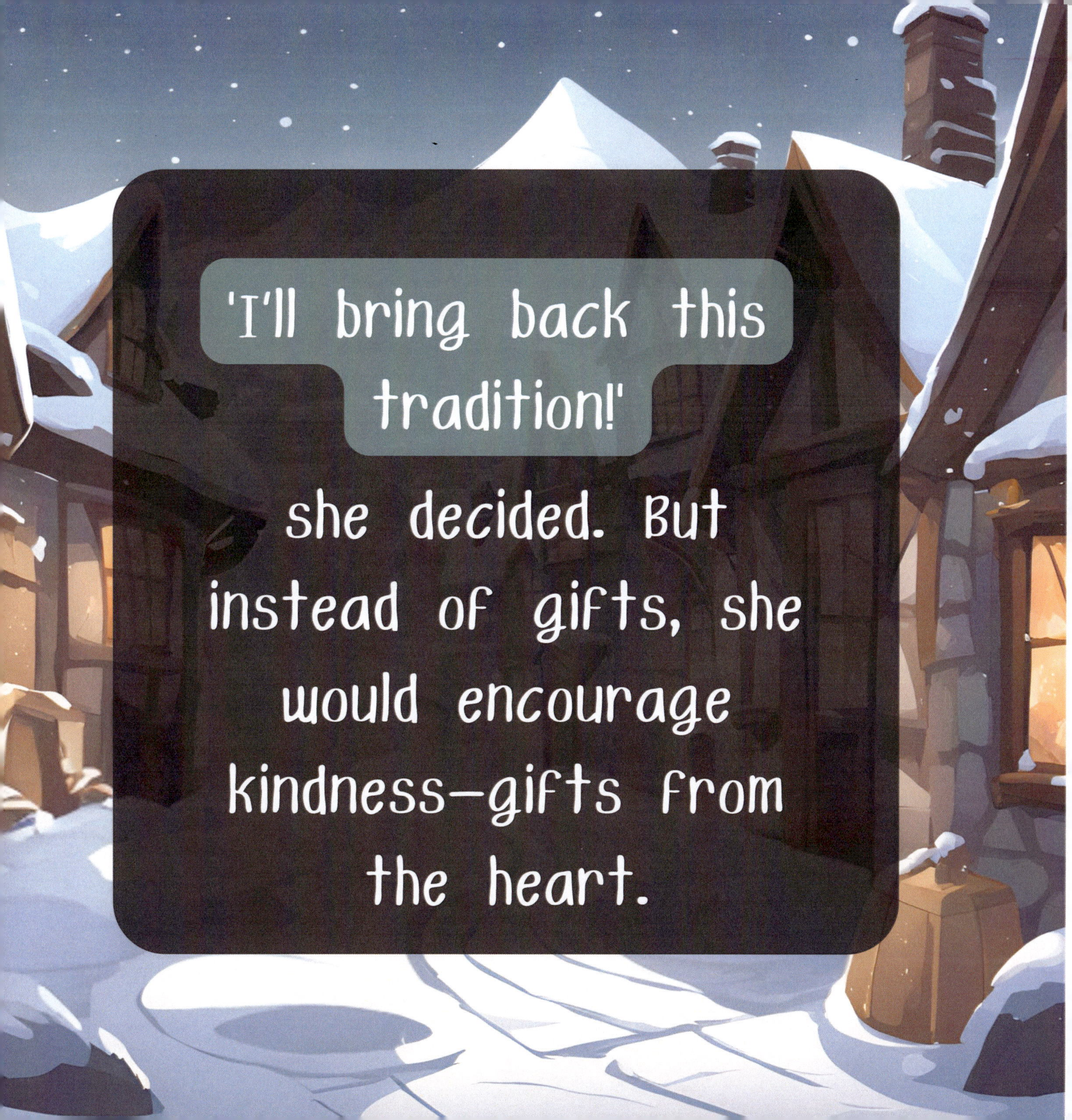

'I'll bring back this tradition!'
she decided. But instead of gifts, she would encourage kindness—gifts from the heart.

As she stepped outside, she found a fox struggling in the snow, his paw injured and unable to walk.

Grateful, the fox wanted to help her spread kindness. Together, they began their journey, with him leading the way.

They soon found a family of rabbits huddled together, shivering in the cold.

'We don't have enough straw to stay warm,' they told her.

Nearby, they found a little pine tree and decided to decorate it with gifts of nature—pinecones, berries, and acorns for their animal friends.

A playful squirrel
watched curiously,
feeling a little lonely.
'Would you like to join
us?' the princess
asked, her kindness
shining brightly.

A wise owl watched
from a nearby branch.

'Christmas is a time for
giving from the heart;'

he said. His words
reminded them of the
true spirit of Christmas.

A gentle deer approached, lost and cold in the snow.
'I don't know the way back,'
she said softly.

Back in the village, the princess led everyone to a tall Christmas tree. Together, they decorated it with handmade ornaments and lit it with glowing candles.

As snow gently fell,
the princess handed
out gifts of
blankets, food, and
holiday cheer to
everyone in need.

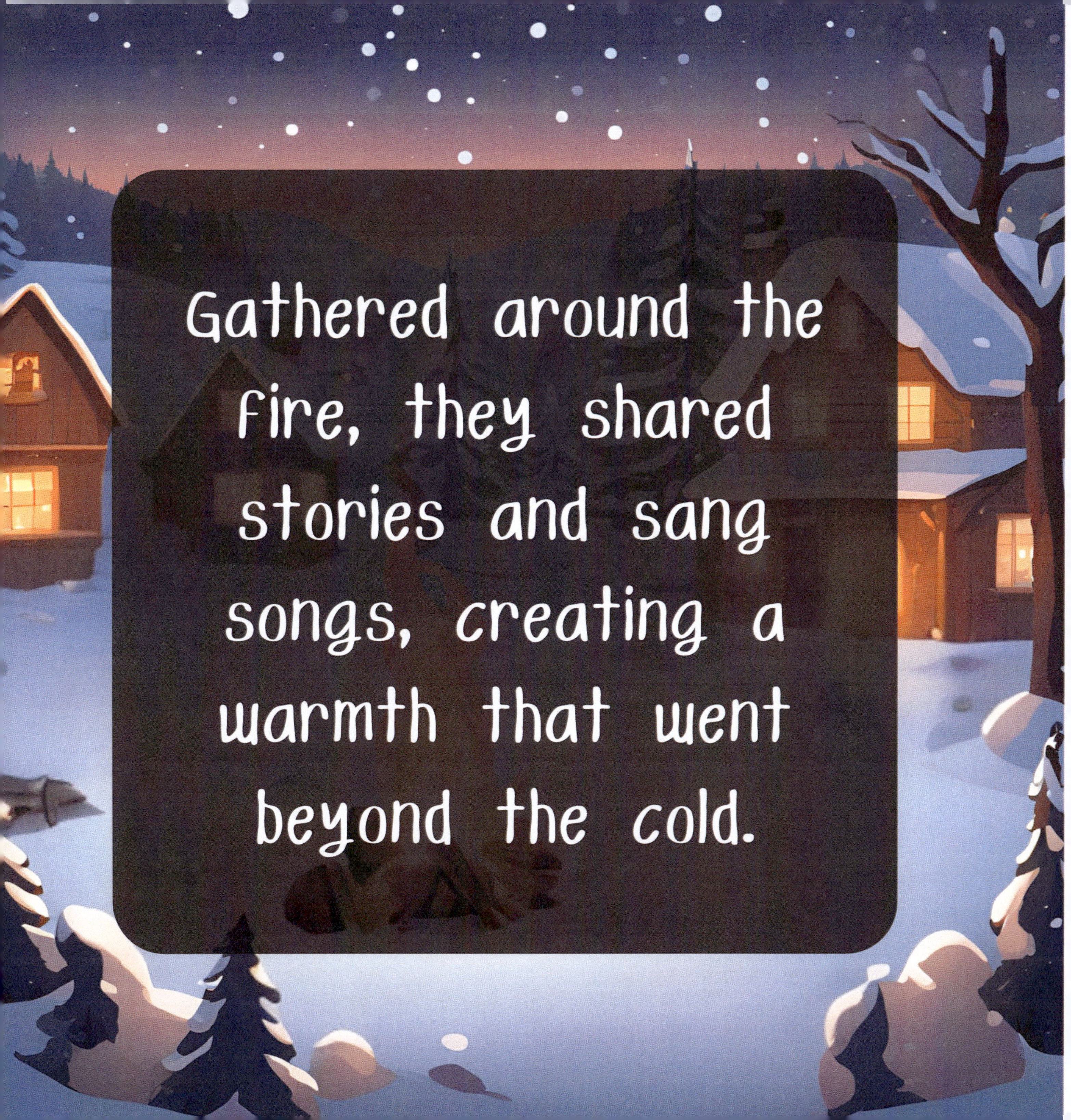
Gathered around the fire, they shared stories and sang songs, creating a warmth that went beyond the cold.

On Christmas morning, the villagers gathered to thank the princess and her animal friends for making this the most heartwarming Christmas ever.

Christmas is not
just about presents,
but about giving
from the heart.
Kindness is the
greatest gift of all.

www.ingramcontent.com/pod-product-compliance
Lightning Source LLC
Chambersburg PA
CBRC090747110726
48005CB00008B/995